GOOD THINKING!
Activity Cards to Reinforce Language and Reasoning Skills

by Kathy Barlow Thurman

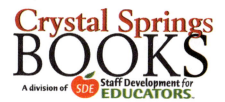

Peterborough, New Hampshire

Published by Crystal Springs Books
A division of Staff Development for Educators (SDE)
10 Sharon Road, PO Box 500
Peterborough, NH 03458
1-800-321-0401
www.crystalsprings.com
www.sde.com

© 2006 Crystal Springs Books
Illustrations © 2006 Crystal Springs Books

Published 2006
Printed in the United States of America
09 08 07 06 05   1 2 3 4 5

ISBN-13: 978-1-884548-88-8
ISBN-10: 1-884548-88-1

Editor: Elaine Ambrose
Art Director, Designer, and Production Coordinator: Soosen Dunholter
Illustrator: Marci McAdam

Crystal Springs Books grants teachers the right to photocopy the reproducibles from this book for classroom use. No other part of this book may be reproduced in whole or in part, or stored in a retrieval system, or transmitted in any form or by any means, electronic, mechanical, photocopying, recording, or otherwise, without written permission of the publisher.

DEDICATION

To my husband, Jeff Thurman, with love.
You are my safe port in every storm.

ACKNOWLEDGMENTS

With much love and thanks to:

My sons, Jason and Josh Sankovitch. When I grow up I want to be just like you (only neater). You have my love, admiration, and respect.

My parents, Claude "Bugs" and Pat Barlow, married for 50 years as of October 1, 2005. Although I'm grown (and middle-aged, yikes!), I rely on you so very often for encouragement and comfort, and you never fail me. Love you.

My sister, Wendy Canterbury. You are a little sister who provides BIG love, support, and excellent phone calls.

My brother, Bruce Barlow. You are proving that it's never too late to set goals and reach them. Go, Bruce!

My Mamaw, Luretha Cross. At the age of 96, you're the very embodiment of the word "spunk." I wish I had your energy.

My husband's family—Betty, George, Lindsey, and Mom Thurman, and Jo Ellen Whitaker. I doubt many other people have in-laws as loving and supportive as you.

My friend and classroom assistant, Gina New. Without your help in the classroom, I would have to pack it up and go home. Really. I value your skills and your friendship.

My friend and fellow kindergarten teacher, Debbie Eads. I couldn't be "in the trenches" with anyone better.

My editor, Elaine Ambrose, thank you for making me sound so good!

TABLE OF CONTENTS

Dear Teacher 6

How to Use the Books of Activity Cards 7

Skills Grid 9

Animal Expressions 11

Draw a Picture with Your Brain 21

Figure It Out 27

Hey! Cut It Out! 41

In Their Shoes 53

It's Your Turn to Teach Me! 61

A Picture Is Worth ONE Word 75

Something's Wrong 87

Switcharoo! 97

To Be . . . or Not to Be 109

What's the Scoop? 119

Words You May Not Say 127

Write Me Back 137

DEAR TEACHER,

If you had to choose one word to describe your school day, I imagine that word would be BUSY. The Energizer Bunny has nothing on teachers! Every day is an endless round of soothing hurt hearts, applying Band-Aids to various body parts, completing paperwork that often seems pointless, and cleaning up spilled milk (or worse)—not to mention actually teaching the children necessary skills. What we do every day is amazing, if you ever get a chance to stop and think about it.

While working with your children, you've noticed that there are skills you'd like to focus on, or areas where you'd like to expand instruction. However, being the busy person you are, you may not have time to develop lessons to do this. This is where I come in: I've created a collection of lessons to supplement language arts instruction and to teach thinking skills, and I'm happy to share them with you. After all, we are united in our dedication to helping children learn, and I believe that teachers should help each other.

There are many reasons why I love these books of activity cards, but one of my very favorite things about them is that they make children STOP and THINK. I feel like I can actually SEE the wheels turning in their brains, and it's an incredible experience. Best of all, children have fun while they learn. And that's the kind of learning that lasts.

Happy Teaching!

Kathy

HOW TO USE THE BOOKS OF ACTIVITY CARDS

Abundant Visual Cues

These 13 books of activity cards are for K–2 children of all ability levels, including English language learners. Most of the activity cards have abundant visual cues to support children who don't yet have a strong language base, and as you know, students make great strides toward becoming readers when they use illustrations to help them decode text. The activities also provide lots of fun while developing language skills, teaching higher level thinking skills, building character, encouraging discussion and problem-solving, and all that important stuff that work sheets and workbooks fail to do.

Easy to Assemble

All of the books included here have been designed and produced to save you time. Just remove each book's pages, laminate them, cut them across the middle, and bind them with metal rings, chicken rings, or another type of removable binding.

Differentiated Lessons

Each book of cards includes an explanation of how to use the book, a "warm-up" lesson, and additional ideas for differentiating instruction. They're user-friendly, too—substitute teachers, classroom assistants, and volunteers will find them manageable and will appreciate having directions and suggestions right at their fingertips.

Flexibility

There are so many ways to use the activity cards:

- with your whole group as sponge or anchor activities to keep them learning during those "between" times
- for guided writing experiences
- with small groups as your lesson for the day
- independently at centers
- and as brainstorming activities to get the children warmed up for the main lesson

From Verbal to Written Responses

Sometimes I use an entire book of activity cards; other times I use only a card or two during a lesson. Initially I have the children give me verbal responses. Later in the year, I ask for written ones. Children love to revisit each book of cards, and you will celebrate the growth they've made.

The text for these activity cards is written above the kindergarten level, so you will need to read them to younger children. If you plan to have children use them independently later, they'll need to hear the text enough times to memorize it, or you can read them the individual card they'll be doing right before letting them go to work independently, so it's fresh in their minds.

Ready, Set, Watch Them Grow!

I encourage you to incorporate these activity cards into your teaching early in the school year. Besides helping you learn about your new students, they'll enable children to get to know each other, setting the tone for a positive and respectful classroom environment.

SKILLS GRID

The skills grid on the facing page provides you with the learning objectives I had in mind for my children as I developed each book and its set of cards. The grid is a handy tool to use when designing your lesson plans, and it's especially helpful for finding a specific skill quickly for children who need more practice in a particular area.

All of these books of activity cards will also

- give young learners experience with the conventions of print
- reinforce the rules for capitalization and punctuation
- provide children with lots of practice following directions
- teach young children to complete tasks
- help students become independent learners
- develop children's self-esteem.

	Animal Expressions	Draw a Picture with Your Brain	Figure It Out	Hey! Cut It Out!	In Their Shoes	It's Your Turn to Teach Me!	A Picture Is Worth ONE Word	Something's Wrong	Switcharoo!	To Be…or Not to Be	What's the Scoop?	Words You May Not Say	Write Me Back
Symbols for words		X		X			X	X		X			
Idioms, similes, metaphors	X			X									
Thought & speech bubbles	X		X		X								
Nouns							X						
Point of view					X	X				X	X		
Personification										X	X		
Stating opinions		X	X	X	X				X	X			
Creative writing	X	X	X		X	X	X	X	X	X	X		X
Social skills & character development	X	X	X	X	X	X	X	X	X	X	X		X
Practical living skills			X	X		X		X		X	X		X
Listening skills	X	X	X	X	X	X	X	X	X	X	X	X	
Creative & critical thinking	X	X	X	X	X	X	X	X	X	X	X	X	
Problem-solving		X	X	X	X	X		X		X	X	X	
Compare & contrast					X					X	X		
Sequencing		X				X							
Sentence completion						X	X		X				X
Comprehension	X	X		X				X					
Home-school connection	X					X					X		X
Research		X								X	X	X	

ANIMAL EXPRESSIONS

Introduce your students to these animal expressions, or figures of speech, to guarantee giggles. While learning the real meanings, children will have fun playing with language and will discover new ways to express themselves. Understanding figures of speech increases their listening and reading comprehension and makes them stronger writers, too.

I'm sick as a dog.

You're in the doghouse.

Hot dog!

This place is going to the dogs.

He's working like a dog.

THE WARM-UP AND THE FIRST LESSON

Tell the children, "Hot dog! I'm as happy as a pig in mud to be teaching you this!" When they stop giggling, tell them that they are going to learn some new and fun ways of saying things. Go over the expressions with them (you may want to do only a couple a day), explaining what each one means. Then encourage your children to use the figures of speech in their daily lives and (for older students) in their writing.

MORE LESSONS TO TEACH USING YOUR BOOK

- This set of cards is great to use to teach speech and thought "bubbles." Invite children to choose their favorite expression and illustrate the animal that goes with it. Then have them write that expression in a speech bubble. In a thought bubble, they will write what the expression means. A child who draws a dog and writes "Hot dog!" in the speech bubble may write "Wow!" or "Great!" in the thought bubble.

- Encourage children to create a new animal expression. Model for them by saying you have decided that when you say, "It's the giraffe's neck!" you really mean that something is very tall. When they are done creating their own expressions, have the children tell the class what their new figure of speech means.

- Families enjoy this homework project: Send a note home telling parents what their children are learning. Ask them to write similar expressions and to explain the meaning of each to their child. At school, children share these with their classmates and you.

- Cut large speech bubbles (12" x 18") from tagboard or poster board. Let the children write favorite expressions on their bubbles. Each child holds the speech bubble next to her head and "reads" it to her classmates.

It's raining cats and dogs.

The cat's got her tongue.

It's the cat's pajamas!

He let the cat
out of the bag.

She's as weak as a kitten.

- -

I like to get up with the chickens.

He's such a mother hen.

There's nobody here but us chickens!

You're a good egg.

Does a chicken have
lips?

I'm going to watch you like a hawk.

I don't want to hear another peep out of you.

This is for the birds.

She's free as a bird.

A little bird told me.

He's happy as a pig in mud.

Pig out!

I'm in hog heaven.

Let's go hog wild!

Hogwash!

This is fine weather for ducks.

That's just ducky.

Lucky duck!

That story gave me goose bumps.

You're on a wild goose chase.

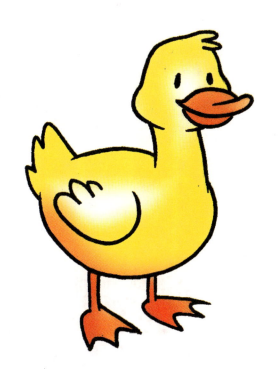

- - - - - - - - - - - - - - - -

You're as sweet as honey.

He's as busy as a bee.

She's got a bee in her bonnet.

He's mad as a hornet.

It's the bee's knees.

I have butterflies
in my stomach.

He wouldn't hurt a fly.

I've got ants
in my pants.

She's snug as a bug in a rug.

He's a real bookworm!

- -

That's a horse of a different color.

He eats like a horse.

Hold your horses.

Quit horsing around.

Wild horses wouldn't
keep me away.

DRAW A PICTURE WITH YOUR BRAIN

Teachers of young children read them books with colorful or interesting artwork. Children also benefit from hearing stories without pictures because this helps them to develop the skill of picturing in their brains what the words are saying. As children grow older, their books have fewer illustrations; we need to prepare them for this. Their comprehension levels will be higher if they have learned to visualize the text they are reading. This is a good time to introduce the term "prior knowledge" if they haven't heard it before. Explain to them that every reader brings her own background of experience, or prior knowledge, to the text she is reading, so everyone's "brain picture" will be different.

On Tuesday the principal came to kindergarten. He played with Play-Doh and dropped the rolling pin on his toe. He built at the block center, but his tower toppled over and blocks went everywhere. He tried making a book, but it kept falling apart. He said, "Wah! Kindergarten is too hard for me." Then he went to the nurse with his sore toe.

THE WARM-UP AND THE FIRST LESSON

Ask the children to open their ears and close their eyes, and tell them that you're going to say some words and you bet they can make a picture in their brain when they hear them. Practice with short phrases such as "a blue bike" or "a soft puppy." Then tell them that you're going to read a short story with no pictures. Their job will be to draw a picture of the story with their brain. Read a story and when you finish, have them draw their "brain pictures." Share everyone's drawings, letting students comment on how the drawings are alike and how they are different.

MORE LESSONS TO TEACH USING YOUR BOOK

- Older students can create short stories without illustrations to read to the group. Have the group (including the teacher) draw their "brain pictures" and share them with the author, who can be a friendly critic and tell each child what was or was not appropriate about his illustrations. Students learn the importance of choosing words carefully and using descriptive language to create a certain picture in their readers' minds.

- Give students practice with the "main idea." Have them say or write titles for the short stories on the book cards and illustrate a book cover for each one.

- Give children some Play-Doh before you read a story aloud. As you read, they shape their dough to represent the mind pictures they're forming of the story. Tactile-kinesthetic learners love this.

- Teach a science lesson about the brain as the control center of the body, and how exercising your brain makes you smarter. Tell students about all the different kinds of "smart," or multiple intelligences. Give older students clipboards (they seem to turn into researchers the minute you put one in their hands) and take them to the library to find one fact about the brain to write or illustrate. Have students share their facts with the class.

It rained and rained. The rain poured down for minutes, and hours, and days. It rained so much that worms made little boats out of leaves so they could float on puddles. Birds had to build roofs on their nests to stay dry. Ladybugs used mushrooms as umbrellas. Finally the rain stopped and there was a beautiful rainbow.

When we went on our field trip, a dog was driving the bus! The regular bus driver was sick, so her dog came to take her place. He said, "Woof!" to all of us, which meant for us to sit down and be quiet on the trip. While he drove, he hung his head out the window. When we got to our destination, he licked us good-bye.

Once we spent the night at school. We got snacks from the cafeteria, we watched a movie in the auditorium, and we played with all our center toys. When we got tired, we took out our nap mats and went to sleep. The next morning when our teacher got to school, we jumped up from our mats and yelled, "Surprise! We're already here!"

Sarah came to school one day in a new jacket. When she tried to take it off, she couldn't because the zipper was stuck! She asked her friends for help, but they couldn't unzip it. She asked her teacher for help, but she couldn't unzip it. She asked the principal for help, but even the principal couldn't unzip it. Sarah got very sweaty so she wiggled out of her jacket without unzipping it. She saved herself!

Blake woke up one morning, looked at the clock, and said, "Yikes! I slept too late and now I'm going to be late for school." He got dressed as fast as he could and hurried to school. As Blake walked down the hallway, people were giggling. When he got to his classroom, his friends started pointing at him and laughing. Blake looked down and saw that he'd put his underwear on OVER his jeans!

It was a sunny day, so the teacher took her wonderful children outside to play on the playground. The children noticed that it looked like someone had been digging in the wood chips. They used their hands to scoop out the chips to see what was under them. They found a treasure chest! When they opened it, they got a BIG surprise.

Andrew was starving, so his mother told him he could order a pizza to be delivered. When the doorbell rang, he answered it. There stood a dinosaur with Andrew's pizza! Andrew yelled, "Mom, there's a dinosaur here with my pizza!" His mom thought he was joking so she said, "Invite him to come in and eat with you," and Andrew did. Boy, did Andrew's mom get a surprise when she came into the kitchen!

One day last summer the ice cream truck broke down. The ice cream man jumped out and yelled, "I'm giving away free ice cream. Everyone come and eat it before it melts!" Boys and girls and moms and dads and grandmas and grandpas all came running. They were holding ice cream sandwiches in each hand and Popsicles with each foot; they even had ice cream cones tucked behind each ear. And supper that night was, you guessed it, ice cream.

I didn't even have a loose tooth, but I wanted the Tooth Fairy to come visit me. I wrote her a note that said, "I have something under my pillow for you," and I put a miniature marshmallow under my pillow to make her think it was my tooth. Then I went to bed. When I woke up the next morning, the marshmallow was gone and the Tooth Fairy had left ME a note. It said, "Thanks for the snack. I'll be back with money when you lose a REAL tooth."

FIGURE IT OUT

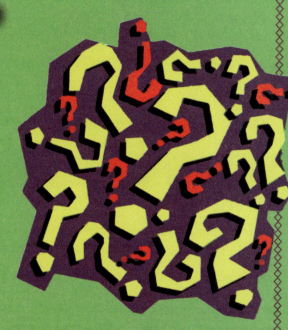

If you're human, there have been times you've been caught in the rain without an umbrella. Being the resourceful problem-solver you are, you grabbed a sack or a newspaper, held it over your head, and ran. This ability to come up with various solutions to a problem is a skill we need to help our children develop for the day when *they* are caught in the rain without an umbrella.

If you don't have a paint smock, how can you keep your clothes clean when you paint?

THE WARM-UP AND THE FIRST LESSON

Right before lunch, tell the children that you have a terrible problem; you forgot your lunch money and you're starving (a melodramatic crying fit at this point will add interest). The children will automatically offer solutions. Resolve the problem together, and thank them for their help. Later, in small group, share the problems in the book with the children and tell them they'll need to use their good brains to solve each one. Encourage them to illustrate and write their solutions, and then share them.

MORE LESSONS TO TEACH USING YOUR BOOK

- This is a great opportunity to teach children simple relaxation exercises for dealing with stress they may feel when faced with a problem. Have them close their eyes (expect peeking) and take several deep breaths. Then tell them to clasp their hands in front of their bodies to center themselves.

- Using role-play, children act out various problems and the class brainstorms whom to go to for a solution or help. For example, if the problem is a toothache, the solution is to go to the dentist. This is a good time to talk about various resources in the community.

- For older students, you can create a problem or have them think of one. They write it on a clipboard and visit various people in the school, asking them what their solutions would be and recording the answers. Back in the room, students share and compare solutions.

- Discuss what "problem" means in a story and introduce the word "plot." Tell the children that as you read aloud they should make a panicked face when they hear the problem being read, and a smiley face when the solution is read. Later, when you're reading aloud, stop when you get to the problem. Ask children to state the problem and to predict possible solutions—a great comprehension skill.

If you don't have an alarm clock, how can you wake up in time for school?

- -

If you don't have a bat, how can you play baseball?

If you don't have any wrapping paper, how can you wrap a gift?

- -

If you don't have a bucket at the beach, how can you move sand from one place to another?

If you don't have a hammer, how can you open a coconut?

If you don't have a sled, how can you go sledding in the snow?

If you don't have a glass, how can you get a drink?

- -

If you don't have a suitcase, how can you carry your clothes when you go on a trip?

If you don't have a mousetrap, how can you catch a mouse?

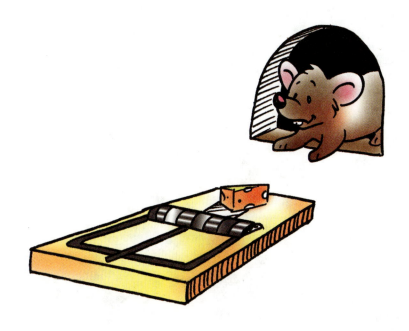

If you don't want to get pinched, how can you pick up a crab?

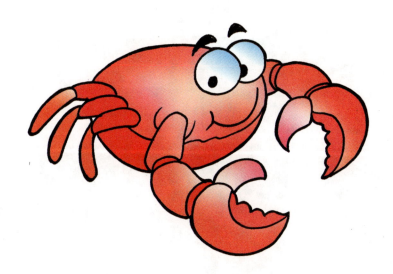

If you don't have an umbrella, how can you stay dry in the rain?

- -

If you want your teacher to smile, how can you behave?

HEY! CUT IT OUT!

At some point during the year, I find that I have many old magazines I need to use up. Putting them out with scissors so children can practice their cutting skills is one solution, but I've added an activity that takes learning a step further by encouraging problem-solving. The children's critical and creative thinking skills are engaged along with their fine-motor skills, and my old magazines get recycled.

Find something that makes an unpleasant sound.

THE WARM-UP AND THE FIRST LESSON

In small group, ask the children to find something that's old. They might point out a beat-up book, their shoes, or their teacher (try not to be offended). Discuss their findings and verbalize how, while they chose different items, all their answers are correct. Next, give each child a magazine and scissors. Tell them to listen carefully—you'll give them a clue from the book and they will search through their magazines for pictures of items that fit that clue. Then they'll cut out the pictures. Compare and contrast the cut-out items and discuss their choices. Be prepared for creative and divergent thinking to emerge!

MORE LESSONS TO TEACH USING YOUR BOOK

- Use this book as a brainstorming think-aloud activity by changing the wording of each page to, "Name something that. . . ." Children shout out answers as they think of them, while you write them on the board.
- Use the title of the book as a springboard for discussing how a phrase or word can have several meanings. Older students can be introduced to the terms "literal" and "figurative." Discuss how "cut it out" literally means to cut something out with scissors, but figuratively it means "stop it." Share other examples and ask children to illustrate them.
- Ask children to use the clues to find items in the classroom that match. For example, "Find something that has four legs" can be answered with "two kids!" or "a table."
- Challenge children to create their own book of clues to use with magazines. To do this, they'll have to think "in reverse" by choosing pictures and then thinking of clues that will work.

Find something that costs no money.

- - - - - - - - - - - - - - - -

Find something you can see through.

Find something that opens and shuts.

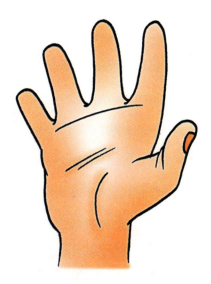

- -

Find something that is hard on the outside and soft on the inside.

Find something that changes
as it grows.

- -

Find something that goes
around and around.

Find something that is used at mealtime.

- -

Find something that is put on top of other things.

Find something that can be turned on and off.

- -

Find something that can be hung up.

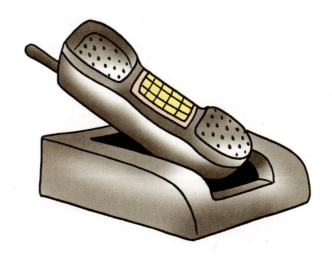

IN THEIR SHOES

Children (and some unpleasant adults best avoided) can be a bit egocentric. To broaden children's minds and perceptions of the world around them, let them practice relating to people or things by putting themselves in another's place, or "in their shoes." Society will thank you for teaching children empathy.

THE WARM-UP AND THE FIRST LESSON

Tell the children they are so smart you're sure that sometimes they can guess what you're thinking. To demonstrate, ask them to yell and jump around, instead of sitting quietly (it'll be a challenge, but they'll rise to the occasion). Look severe and pained as chaos reigns. Then ask them what you might be thinking. Of course, they'll say you're thinking you wish they'd settle down, or that you had some earplugs. Sketch yourself on the board with thought bubbles and record their ideas.

Next, give each child a card, asking him to put himself "in the shoes" of each person or object pictured. Children say or write what each object or person might be thinking. When they can perceive what others may be thinking, children create more interesting characters in their writing. Now you've taught them point of view.

MORE LESSONS TO TEACH USING YOUR BOOK

- Explain the meaning of "in your shoes." Have children remove their shoes (you, too!) and trade with a partner. They slip on their partner's shoes as best they can, and say or write what they think that child thinks about, or what it's like to be that child.
- Take photos of staff at school—a cafeteria worker, the principal, a bus driver, and custodian. Display them on a bulletin board, surrounded by thought bubbles. Invite children to write what each might be thinking.
- Introduce older students to personification. Ask them what the pencil sharpener in their classroom might think or feel. If it could speak, what might it say? Children enjoy writing short pieces from the perspective of an inanimate object.
- Help children learn empathy, essential to character development, by discussing how people may think things that they don't say aloud because they might hurt another's feelings or make them angry. Children illustrate themselves with a thought bubble and a speech bubble. In the thought bubble, they write something they wouldn't say aloud, such as, "You're hogging the toys." In the speech bubble, they write more appropriate words to say aloud, such as, "I wish you'd share the toys."

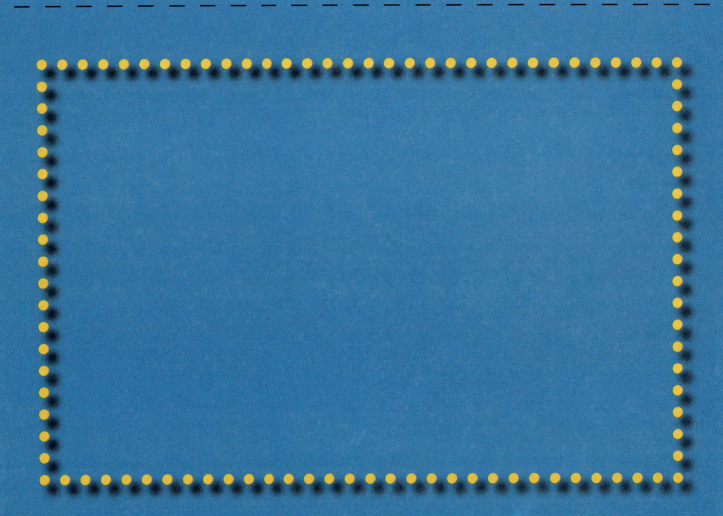

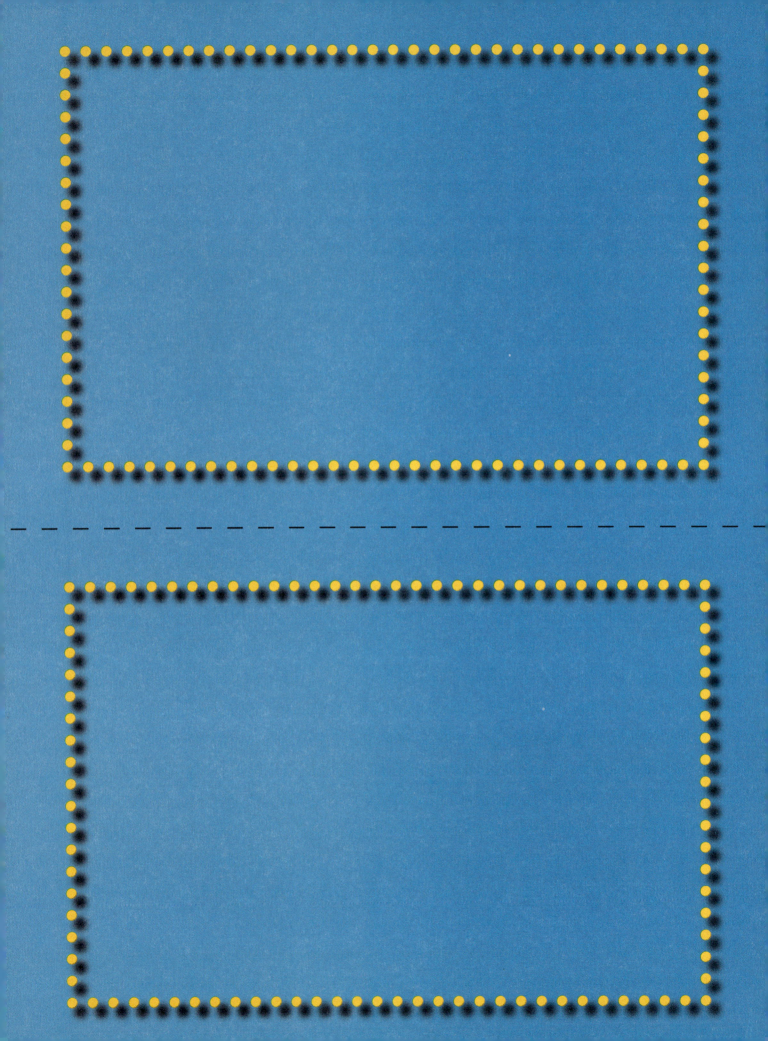

IT'S YOUR TURN TO TEACH ME!

In my classroom, the children take turns being "Today's Teacher." That child wears a special hat, tells the other children what to do (and how to do it, within reason!), and sits in my chair (oh, the heady feeling of power). They eagerly anticipate their turn to be in charge. This book activity allows children to experience the pleasure of teaching someone how to do something while they practice writing step-by-step instructions. The "without" condition gives children the added challenge of problem-solving.

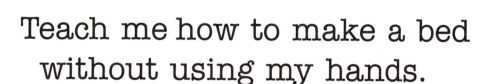

Teach me how to make a bed without using my hands.

THE WARM-UP AND THE FIRST LESSON

Bring a toy to school that you think most of the children are familiar with and tell them that you don't know how to play with it. Ask them to tell you how to use the toy and record every step of their instructions. The children love being more knowledgeable than their teacher and feel very proud to be helping her learn how to do something. After all, it's usually the other way around!

MORE LESSONS TO TEACH USING YOUR BOOK

- Let the children work in pairs to act out the "how to" situation they will write about. Have them stop after each step and write it down before going on to act out the next step. This will break the process down, making it easier for them to manage.

- Give the children the sentence frame "Teach me how to _____ without _____" and challenge them to think of a writing experience for you to do! Let the children evaluate your written response and give you a grade.

- Bake a cake together. (Check with your school nurse first about any food allergies your children may have.) Show them the step-by-step instructions on the back of the cake mix box (who bakes from scratch anymore?) and follow the directions together. After the cake cools, frost it and eat it, of course. Be sure to treat yourself!

- Send a note home to parents telling them their child is responsible for teaching the class how to do something they're good at, such as telling knock-knock jokes, blowing bubblegum bubbles, turning a cartwheel, etc. The parents help their child practice their "how to" lesson and the child teaches it to the class on her assigned day. This is a great self-esteem booster for the child doing the teaching and lots of fun for everyone else.

Teach me how to play outside
without getting dirty.

Teach me how to pull a loose tooth
without using my fingers.

Teach me how to have fun at school without breaking any rules.

Teach me how to ride a bike without having a wreck.

Teach me how to swing really high without being pushed.

Teach me how to make someone laugh without tickling them.

Teach me how to get the teacher's attention without saying anything.

Teach me how to go to bed at night without being afraid of the dark.

Teach me how to remember to do homework without being reminded.

Teach me how to give my parents a gift without spending any money.

Teach me how to roller-skate
without falling down.

- -

Teach me how to frost a cupcake
without using a knife.

A PICTURE IS WORTH ONE WORD

The teacher loves ice cream.

    I believe I first heard the word "noun" when I was in middle school, but times have changed, of course, and now we introduce nouns in kindergarten. To help children get the idea that a noun names a person, place, or thing, let them experience writing rebus sentences because they can actually draw a picture to represent the noun(s).

A princess put on a crown of flowers.

A ____ put on a _____ of ____.

THE WARM-UP AND THE FIRST LESSON

In small group, ask the children to draw themselves, their house, and a favorite toy. Then ask them to draw "the." You'll see gaping mouths and hear giggles of confusion. Ask them what picture they get in their minds of the word "the," and they'll say they don't get one. Help them to see that's why they can't draw it, explaining that people, places, and things are nouns and you can draw a picture of each. Now read a rebus book to the children, and discuss how pictures take the place of some of the words—the nouns. Tell them that they are going to write rebus sentences, or sentences that have both words and drawings.

MORE LESSONS TO TEACH USING YOUR BOOK

- Let the children make lift-the-flap books with a picture on the flap and the noun underneath. Have them exchange papers and try to guess what noun the picture represents before they lift the flap.
- Play "noun charades." Children take turns acting out people, places, or things. For people, they might choose to be a baby, a cheerleader, or the teacher (always good for laughs). For places, they might act out being in the shower, at school, or at the zoo. Or they might act out a thing—a dog, a butterfly, or scissors. Have each child tell the group whether she's a person, place, or thing.
- Lend the children (with supervision) a digital camera to take photos of nouns they find at school. Attach the prints to chart paper or poster board, and ask the children to construct sentences around the photos, using the pictures to illustrate the nouns. Instead of a digital camera, you might use disposable cameras or magazine pictures.
- Play a game I call "noun, not noun." Tell your children that if you say a noun, such as tree, they should stand up, turn around, and sit back down. If it isn't a noun, they stay seated. Naturally, they'll want to hear more nouns than "not nouns."

The monster made the boy and girl scream.

The ___ made the ___ and ___ scream.

- -

A cow jumped over the moon and landed on a star.

A ___ jumped over the ___ and landed on a ___.

There were fish swimming in the boy's bathtub.

There were _____ swimming in the boy's _____.

- -

A bird wearing a parachute fell out of its nest.

A ____ wearing a ____ fell out of its ____.

The bee stung the baby on the nose.

The ____ stung the ____ on the ____.

- -

The girl played in the rain with a duck.

The ____ played in the ____ with a ____.

A dog and cat licked ice cream cones.

A _____ and _____ licked _____.

- -

A whale went down the slide at the swimming pool.

A _____ went down the _____ at the _____.

The teacher took the children to hunt for bugs.

The _____ took the _____ to hunt for _____.

- -

The monkey ate a banana in a tree.

The _____ ate a _____ in a _____.

SOMETHING'S WRONG

Recently, on the playground in front of my children, I said to my aide, "I'm going to run back inside and get my camera. Or do you want *me* to?" Of course, my aide knew that I meant, "Or do *you* want to?" and that I was just a bit rattled (imagine that). The children, however, took great delight in pointing out my mistake and correcting me. This activity will sharpen your children's listening and critical-thinking skills, along with introducing them to taking notes.

I planted some flower seeds in my garden and watered them. Now I have flowers growing on my head.

Whenever my dog wants to have his tummy rubbed he says, "Meow."

THE WARM-UP AND THE FIRST LESSON

Gather the children together and say, "If you want to go to the playground, raise your *feet*." The children will gleefully say, "Feet! You mean hands!" and some wise guys will actually raise their feet, of course. Then tell them that for this activity they are going to get to correct your mistakes. They will listen to a sentence or brief story and use their ears to hear what you say *wrong*. The additional challenge for them is that they're going to make a note of what you said wrong, rather than blurting it out. For example, if at snack time you said, "Who wants chocolate water?" the children would quickly draw a glass or write the word, according to their ability level. Then share everyone's efforts.

MORE LESSONS TO TEACH USING YOUR BOOK

- Make good use of your old magazines by having the children combine pictures they've cut out to make a humorous illustration and have them write a "wrong" sentence or story about it.

- Challenge the children to illustrate your wrong sentence or story and extend it to make it even sillier, or more wrong. Tell them you expect to laugh a lot when you read it.

- Give each child paper and pencil and encourage them to take notes during an educational video. Tell them that they should write or draw whatever they see *during* the video that is important to them. Of course, they won't come anywhere near mastering this skill, but it's good to introduce the skill early. When the video ends, let students share their "notes." This gives you a chance to assess your students' ability to prioritize information, too.

- Explain why people sometimes say the wrong word(s); sometimes it's because they have a lot on their minds and are distracted, or they are thinking faster than they speak. Tell the children that it's generally not considered good manners for them to correct adults, but it's okay this time because they are working to become better listeners.

One day I went out on the lake in a boat.
When I got home, there was a
fish sitting on my couch.

I put ketchup and mustard on my hot dog
and then my hot dog bit me.

Scrambled eggs are my favorite
toy to play with.

My grandmother is very old.
We gave her a birthday party with cake
and ice cream. She turned six years old.

Playing sports is lots of fun.
My favorite sports are soccer
and pancakes.

I got dirty playing on the playground at school, so I went home and took a bath in chocolate milk.

I'm going to be a baby when
I grow up.

It took me a long time and a lot of practice to learn how to count, but now I can count all the way to z.

I like to look nice, so I get a haircut when my hair is too short.

My mom and I bought groceries. When we got home, she put the ice cream in the oven.

- -

I don't want to get cavities, so I brush my hair every morning and every night before I go to bed.

The rain and the sun made the grass in my yard grow very tall, so I mowed the lawn with my bike.

Sometimes when I play hard, I get hot and thirsty. Then I drink a glass of spaghetti and meatballs to cool me off.

I had to sharpen my book after I wrote a long story on my paper.

Books are my favorite things. When I look at the pictures and read the words, I turn the pages with my toes.

When it's dark at night, I look up and see the sun and the stars in the sky, and I make a wish.

SWITCHAROO!

Children stretch their brains when they learn to compare and contrast; they're using logic and reasoning abilities, as well as creative and critical thinking. For this activity, they'll look at things one way and then, "Switcharoo!"—they'll look again from a different perspective. As part of this learning process, they will work in pairs, talk to one another, and get up and move—all activities at which our children excel (☺).

1. Write   2. Discuss   3. Switcharoo!

I think they are alike because...

I think they are different because...

THE WARM-UP AND THE FIRST LESSON

Ask for two volunteers to stand in front of the group. Challenge the rest of the children to brainstorm how the two are alike and how they're different. Next, pair the children and have them sit beside each other with a card in front of them. The child on the left of the card does "alike" and the child on the right does "different." Together they look at the items on the card and write (or say) their answers and then discuss them. Then, "Switcharoo!"—they switch places so the child who did "alike" now does "different," and vice versa. From this new perspective, children write, or say, an answer for the "other" side.

MORE LESSONS TO TEACH USING YOUR BOOK

- Have the children stand to play this game. Once the excitement dies down, tell them that when you shout, "Alike!" they must move exactly like you (if you're hopping, they hop, too). When you shout, "Different!" they move in some way different from you. Play until you're worn out.
- Give each child a sheet of paper with her picture photocopied on it twice to look like identical twins. Each child writes a story about her twin, including her name, favorite food, how she acts, and other personal characteristics.
- Let children bring a favorite toy from home and pair up with a friend to discuss or write about how their toys are alike and different. This is a good time to introduce young learners to Venn diagrams.
- Pair the children and give each child the same set of Legos or other blocks. Pairs sit back to back and build something. Then they turn around to compare and contrast the end products. Next, challenge them to build objects that match exactly, without looking at each other's work. One child builds an object and then tells her partner exactly how to build the same structure, using words only (no peeking!). They'll practice giving and following directions and using precise, descriptive language. When they're done, they switch roles. It's challenging, but great fun, and children will want to do it again and again.

1. Write   2. Discuss   3. Switcharoo!

I think they are alike because...   I think they are different because...

---

1. Write   2. Discuss   3. Switcharoo!

 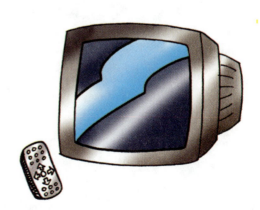

I think they are alike because...   I think they are different because...

1. Write   2. Discuss   3. Switcharoo!

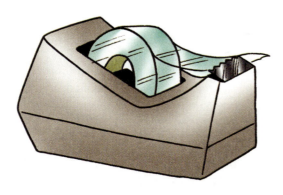 

I think they are alike because...   I think they are different because...

---

1. Write   2. Discuss   3. Switcharoo!

I think they are alike because...   I think they are different because...

1. Write   2. Discuss   3. Switcharoo!

I think they are alike because...

I think they are different because...

---

1. Write   2. Discuss   3. Switcharoo!

I think they are alike because...

I think they are different because...

1. Write   2. Discuss   3. Switcharoo!

I think they are alike because...   I think they are different because...

- -

 1. Write   2. Discuss   3. Switcharoo!

I think they are alike because...   I think they are different because...

1. Write   2. Discuss   3. Switcharoo!

I think they are alike because...

I think they are different because...

---

 1. Write   2. Discuss   3. Switcharoo!

I think they are alike because...

I think they are different because...

TO BE. . .OR NOT TO BE

When I choose a child to be "Today's Teacher," that child experiences not only the exhilaration of being in charge (☺) but also the responsibility involved. Today's Teacher must serve the snack to everyone else first, hold the door to the playground until all the children are out, and do all my paperwork (just kidding). In other words, he sees some of the pros and cons of being a teacher. This book gives children practice seeing the pros and cons of being various people or objects (personification, anyone?).

I would like to be a tree because...

I would not like to be a tree because...

THE WARM-UP AND THE FIRST LESSON

Take the children outside and gather around a tree. Let them touch the tree, smell its leaves, and lie down under it. Ask them if they would like to be trees, inviting them to tell you things they would and would not like about it. Then, back inside, continue the lesson by allowing the children to act like whatever is on the page you've given them. Later, have them say, draw, and/or write what they would and wouldn't like about being that person or object.

MORE LESSONS TO TEACH USING YOUR BOOK

- Explain that the recognized symbol for "no" is a red circle with a line from the upper left to the lower right. Let them talk about where they've seen such signs, and what they meant, eliciting that whatever is in the circle is forbidden, or banned. Ask children to make their own signs with this symbol (and expect the most popular one to show brothers or sisters under the red line!).

- Brainstorm what the opposite of the "no" symbol would be, and together create a "yes" symbol, such as thumbs up or a smiley face. Ask students to invent their own symbols for "yes."

- Introduce your children to debating by explaining that it's a discussion of both sides of an issue. Divide them into a "for" and an "against" group and let them debate topics of interest to them, such as, "Children should drink chocolate milk at breakfast."

- Show children how writers sometimes use different styles of print, or fonts, to make us feel a certain way. Send them to the class library to hunt for children's books with changes in font. Share what they find by reading some of these; ask them why they think the author or illustrator wanted the words to look different. This builds confidence in children who aren't yet reading; they're looking for font changes within text, and they don't need to decode…yet! Invite them to write words in styles to match the meanings, such as shaky letters for "cold," or "love" in curly, pink letters. This also helps English language learners build vocabulary.

I would like to
be a baby
because...

I would not like to
be a baby
because...

- -

I would like to
be a robot
because...

I would not like to
be a robot
because...

I would like to be a wizard because...

I would not like to be a wizard because...

I would like to be an ant because...

I would not like to be an ant because...

I would like to be a dolphin because...

I would not like to be a dolphin because...

I would like to be a shoe because...

I would not like to be a shoe because...

I would like to be a monkey because...

I would not like to be a monkey because...

I would like to be a parent because...

I would not like to be a parent because...

WHAT'S THE SCOOP?

When police officers, veterinarians, and other speakers come to visit our school, they usually end their talks by asking the children if they have any questions. Hands shoot up and when called on, often the child makes a remark such as "My dog died," instead of asking a question. This book helps children to practice asking questions that are on topic and introduces them to the concept that most questions start with the words who, what, when, where, why, or how.

Interview a farmer.

WHO? WHAT? WHEN? WHERE? WHY? HOW?

THE WARM-UP AND THE FIRST LESSON

Say, "I'm going to ask you a question. Put on your elephant ears so you're ready to answer." When you have their attention say, "I like bugs." They'll sit with the usual wiggles and look at you. After several silent seconds, explain that they didn't feel a need to answer because what you said was a statement, not a question. Then say, "What bugs can you name?" Hands will shoot up, and after they've had a chance to give answers, explain that because it was a question, they felt the need to answer. Explain that most questions begin with who, what, where, when, why, or how, letting them give examples of each. Then let them choose a person from the cards to write interview questions for. The illustrations will serve as prompts to help them stay on topic and think of interesting questions. Challenge them to say or write a question for each word listed on the page.

MORE LESSONS TO TEACH USING YOUR BOOK

- Role-play for children an interview with your aide (here's your chance to ham it up!). Then give them a chance to be TV stars as you videotape them interviewing each other. Before the interviews, pairs of children discuss and write questions. Give the interviewer a microphone for the full effect!
- Ask children to imagine careers for animals: Would a fish be a good swim instructor? Would a dog make a good police officer, or a cat a good spy? Let children choose an animal to write about and illustrate in the appropriate uniform or setting.
- Ask students questions that require research to answer, such as, "How many kinds of sharks are there?" Take them to your school library to find answers.
- For homework, have children interview a family member, using the question words they've practiced and recording it on paper or tape. Share interviews with the class.

Interview a racecar driver.

WHO? WHAT? WHEN? WHERE? WHY? HOW?

Interview a principal.

WHO? WHAT? WHEN? WHERE? WHY? HOW?

Interview a veterinarian.

WHO? WHAT? WHEN? WHERE? WHY? HOW?

Interview a police officer.

WHO? WHAT? WHEN? WHERE? WHY? HOW?

Interview a firefighter.

WHO? WHAT? WHEN? WHERE? WHY? HOW?

Interview a hairdresser.
WHO? WHAT? WHEN? WHERE? WHY? HOW?

WORDS YOU MAY NOT SAY

Educational research shows that the more experience children have using language, the better their literacy skills are. While children love to talk and have many interesting things to say, we need to help them develop their descriptive skills as well as their conversational ones. This book is fun for them because it challenges their brains in a game-like format, encouraging them to think of new ways to describe familiar things.

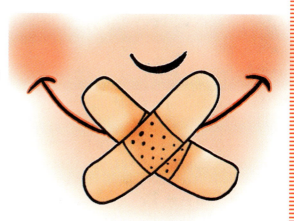

Describe a **tree**.

You may not say these words:

tree, green, or leaves.

THE WARM-UP AND THE FIRST LESSON

Have one child stand up, and tell the group that you're going to describe this child without using his name, hair color, or age, and then do so. Next, choose a card from this set and, without letting the children see it, describe the object pictured without using the three "off-limits" words. Children guess what it could be until someone is correct. That child stands in front of the group with you. Show her a picture of what she's to describe, whisper to her the three words she may not say, and tell her you'll say, "Beep!" if she accidentally uses one. The child describes the object until another student guesses correctly and takes her place. Play continues until the teacher is worn out.

MORE LESSONS TO TEACH USING YOUR BOOK

- Make a word web, letting children call out descriptive words for the object in the middle of the web.
- Give each child paper to draw an object and help him list the three words that he wants to challenge the other children not to say. For example, if he draws a boat, he might list the words "boat," "water," and "float" for the words classmates can't use to describe a boat. Let the children take turns doing the activity with one another.
- Give each child some Play-Doh. Start describing an object and have them listen to your clues to shape it. For example, you may be thinking of a worm. You'll say, "It's long and thin," and wait for the children to shape their Play-Doh that way. Then say, "Both ends look the same." Continue giving clues until a child guesses what they're making.
- Introduce children to a word they're unfamiliar with to describe their object, and show them how to use the dictionary to find the word and its meaning. They'll need help, of course, but it will introduce them to the dictionary in a fun way.

Describe a **birthday cake**.

You may not say these words:

 birthday, cake, or eat.

Describe a **dinosaur**.

You may not say these words:

 dinosaur, fossil, or extinct.

Describe a **snowman**.

You may not say these words:

 snowman, cold, or melt.

Describe a **school bus**.

You may not say these words:

 bus, school, or driver.

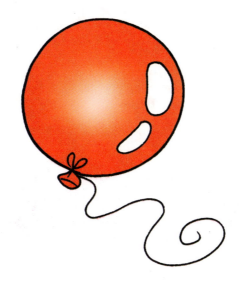

Describe a **balloon**.

You may not say these words:

 balloon, blow up, or string.

- -

Describe a **rainbow**.

You may not say these words:

 rainbow, clouds, or arch.

Describe a **star**.

You may not say these words:

 star, twinkle, or millions.

- -

Describe a **rabbit**.

You may not say these words:

 rabbit, bunny, or hop.

WRITE ME BACK

Everyone likes to receive a personal note; think how excited you feel when you get a letter from someone you care about. Often when our children write in the classroom, they are giving us information, but they don't get anything personally fulfilling in return for their efforts (stickers and smiley faces... ho, hum). A wonderful way to encourage your students to write is to write them back. For example, if they write to you about a special wish they'd like to have come true, you respond to their comments and add what you'd wish for. It makes them feel so important to receive an answer from you, and it helps everyone get to know each other better.

A secret I have is...

Thanks for sharing. I'll write you back!

THE WARM-UP AND THE FIRST LESSON

Come to small group covered with pencils—behind your ears, in your pockets, a pencil on yarn around your neck, and more tied to your shoelaces. The children will want to know the point (a little pun) of all those pencils. Tell them they are going to write to you, and since you'll write back to them, you'll need lots of pencils. Then let them choose a page from the book and write you a letter, using the sentence starter. They give you their letter and you write each child back. I write back the next day, so children don't have to wait long for an answer. So you're not overwhelmed, limit the number of children who may write to you each day by choosing one reading group to write one day, and another the next. Let children try to read your responses alone first, then help with unfamiliar words. And just you watch—they'll write you back again!

MORE LESSONS TO TEACH USING YOUR BOOK

- Make blank "Write Me Back" books for each child by folding paper in half crosswise (hamburger style) and stapling it along the folded side. The children and you can write each other in these books (with topics suggested here or your own). When the books are full, the children take them home to read and reread. Some students may even begin writing to each other.

- If children write a simple question (such as "Do you like red?"), write a detailed answer rather than "yes" or "no." Discuss which type of answer they prefer to receive. Let them practice adding details to their answers to simple questions you have asked them.

- To help children remember that sentences start with an uppercase letter, have spaces between the words, and end with punctuation, put three dots on the back of their hands with washable marker. After they've written their sentence, they check it by touching each dot to see if they've remembered all three.

- Ask staff at school to participate in the Write Me Back activity. The children love writing to the custodian, principal, or school nurse, and receiving answers.

- For a summer writing project, give each child a few addressed, stamped postcards for writing to you. Then, of course, write them back! Be sure to take their addresses with you before you leave for summer vacation.

I am scared of...

Thanks for sharing. I'll write you back!

- -

The best gift I ever got was...

Thanks for sharing. I'll write you back!

The funniest thing I ever saw was....

Thanks for sharing. I'll write you back!

- -

If I could drive, I would...

Thanks for sharing. I'll write you back!